★ THE CAPITA[illegible]

WASHINGTON

"Wherever the American citizen may be a stranger, he is at home here."—FREDERICK DOUGLASS

L'ENFANT'S CITY

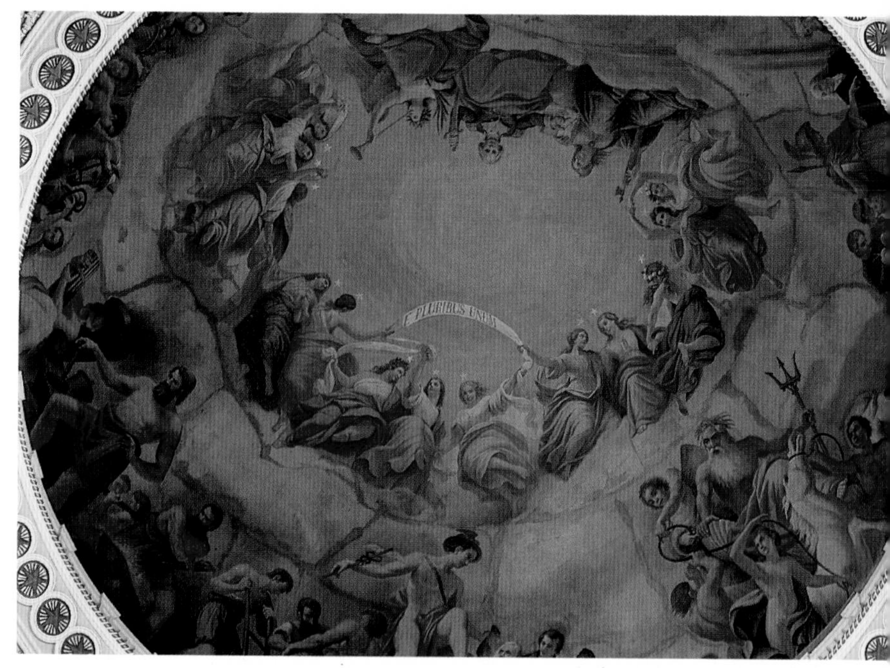

EYE OF THE CAPITOL DOME. *Italian immigrant Constantino Brumidi spent twenty-five years decorating the Capitol's interior. His fresco* Apotheosis of Washington *depicts the first president surrounded by allegorical figures.*

When George Washington selected Major Pierre Charles L'Enfant to plan the new nation's capital, the thirty-six-year-old military engineer envisioned broad avenues, majestic vistas, and spacious parks. In 1791, when no modern nation had ever planned the construction of its capital, L'Enfant conceived of a city, as he wrote to Washington, "magnificent enough to grace a great nation."

Unfortunately, his expenditures were as extravagant as his vision. When L'Enfant presented a bill for $95,500 to a Congress that had decided to pay no more than $3,000, he was dismissed from his post, and the uncompromising engineer died in poverty.

For many years L'Enfant's plan looked as if it might suffer a similar fate. Transforming a remote marshland into a city of classical elegance was far from simple. L'Enfant's ideas were implemented so slowly that while his original plan wisely specified separate housing for the government's legislative, executive, and judicial branches, the Supreme Court was relegated to cramped chambers in the Capitol until 1935.

The legislative and executive branches fared better. Despite financial difficulties, construction on the Capitol Building and the President's House was under way by 1800, the year the federal government moved to the new city. Fourteen years later, during the War of 1812, both buildings were gutted when the British burned Washington, a calamity that might have been averted had Congress considered the tiny capital a likely target for attack. A thunderstorm saved Washington from complete destruction, a coat of white paint disguised scorch marks on the President's House, construction of the Capitol recommenced, and Congress voted, by a narrow margin, to stay in the capital city.

Still, when Charles Dickens visited Washington in 1842, he was not impressed. At that time, it was considered a diplomatic hardship post—an easy target for European wits like Dickens, who dubbed the capital "City of Magnificent Intentions." Washington's early history indicates that Dickens's opinion may have been warranted. During the Civil War, the city's muddy streets and parks were filled with soldiers. The halls of Congress served as a bivouac for 3,000 troops and later as a 1,500-cot hospital. Yet in the midst of this suffering, Abraham Lincoln decided that construction on the Capitol should continue. "If people see the Capitol going on," he stated, "it is a sign we intend the Union shall go on." Like L'Enfant, Lincoln recognized the importance of Washington as a symbol to the nation and the world, and so, on December 2, 1863, the nine-million-pound, cast-iron Capitol dome was crowned with the Statue of Freedom.

As the United States gained international prominence in the years following World War I, so too did its capital, and today, the Capitol dome gleams above one of the most important cities in the world. Washington is now more highly populated than the entire country was during L'Enfant's lifetime. Yet L'Enfant's influence endures, most obviously in the city's system of avenues running diagonally across a grid of streets to connect key sites, in the circles where these avenues intersect, and in the placement of the Capitol, the White House, and the Washington Monument. While contemporary Washington does not reflect the letter of L'Enfant's plan, it certainly reflects the spirit, and true to his vision, it graces the nation magnificently.

ROTUNDA FRIEZE, THE CAPITOL. *While he was working on this frieze, Brumidi's scaffold slipped; the seventy-two-year-old artist clung to the platform for almost twenty minutes until help arrived. Badly shaken, he was unable to continue the project and died four months later.*

SUPREME COURT BUILDING. *Designed by Cass Gilbert, it is probably the largest marble structure in the world, so massive that when the justices moved into their new chambers, one suggested, "We ought to ride over on elephants."*

IMENT, SUPREME URT BUILDING. *icted with three allegori- figures are Chief Justices rshall, Taft, and Hughes, yer Elihu Root, the build- 's architect, Cass Gilbert, d the sculptor himself, bert Aitken—all anachro- tically clad in togas.*

XECUTIVE OFFICE BUILDING. *Its ten acres of floor space now contain White House staff fices and the Office of Management and Budget. In 1913, then captain Douglas lacArthur added concrete planters to brighten the baroque façade.*

THOMAS JEFFERSON BUILDING, LIBRARY OF CONGRESS. *Founded in 1800 with a budget of $5,000, the Library of Congress is now believed to be the largest single repository of information in the world. Among the collection's over eighty-three million objects are a Gutenberg Bible, the contents of Lincoln's pockets on the night of his assassination, and the scrapbooks of magician Harry Houdini. Free music and literary programs, exhibits, and guided tours are available.*

FOUNTAIN, LIBRARY OF CONGRESS. *The energetic bronze sculpture by Roland Hinton Perry depicts Neptune surrounded by his court and occupies a fifty-foot semicircular pool on the Library's west front. The central figure is twice life-size.*

STATUARY HALL, THE CAPITOL. *This hall was established when Congress invited each state to donate statues of two of its distinguished citizens. More than fifty eight- to ten-ton statues proved too heavy for the floor, and in the 1930s the rest were placed elsewhere in the building.*

OLD SUPREME COURT CHAMBER, THE CAPITOL *(Facing). This small chamber with its unusual half-dome ceiling was occupied by the Senate from 1800 to 1810 and by the Supreme Court from 1810 to 1860. It was so crowded that the justices were compelled to robe in front of spectators.*

WHITE HOUSE. *The oldest public building in Washington did not officially receive its current name until the 1910s. James Hoban's original design for the President's House, based on Leinster House in Dublin, was selected through a competition to which Thomas Jefferson submitted an anonymous entry. The North Portico, designed by Benjamin Latrobe, was added to the building in 1829.*

OVAL OFFICE. *Refurnished to each new occupant's taste, it is located in the West Wing, an office complex directly connected to the executive mansion. Some presidents have preferred to use the Oval Office only on formal occasions, doing most of their work in a small nearby study.*

John Q. Adams State Drawing Room, State Department Building. *Furnished with American antiques of the period from 1740 to 1825, this is one of several rooms where the president, vice president, and Cabinet members entertain prominent world figures.*

SHERIDAN CIRCLE. *The bronze statue near Embassy Row depicts General Philip H. Sheridan on his favorite horse, Rienzi. It was designed by Gutzon Borglum, who also designed the Mount Rushmore sculptures.*

PEACOCK ALLEY, WILLARD HOTEL. *The original 1818 hotel was razed at the turn of the century and replaced with a twelve-story Beaux Arts building, now fully renovated. Charles Dickens stayed at the Willard in 1842; Julia Ward Howe wrote "The Battle Hymn of the Republic" here in 1861.*

OLD PENSION BUILDING *(Facing). Built as a memorial to Civil War veterans, it now houses the National Building Museum. These massive Roman-style columns, plastered and painted to simulate marble, are made of approximately 85,000 bricks each. Many inaugural balls have been held here in the city's largest room.*

METRO STATION. *Washington's 103-mile rapid rail system combines modern technology with classical elegance. The stations' coffered ceilings were inspired by the Pantheon in Rome.*

DULLES INTERNATIONAL AIRPORT *(Facing). This airport, named for John Foster Dulles, secretary of state during the Eisenhower administration, was dedicated in 1962. The terminal, by Eero Saarinen, is a masterpiece of modern architecture.*

MUSEUMS AND THE MALL

SMITHSONIAN BUILDING *(Above and facing). Designed by James Renwick, Jr., the "Castle" houses James Smithson's tomb and the Institution's administrative offices.*

To some the red sandstone Smithsonian Building may seem as out of place among the marble, glass, and concrete structures that line the mile-long Washington Mall as the life-size fiberglass triceratops in front of the Museum of Natural History. The Smithsonian Building, a small Romanesque structure known as the "Castle," completed in 1855 when the rest of the Mall was still a tangle of railroad tracks and shanties, was built with funds bequeathed by an Englishman to a country he had never seen. James Smithson's hope was "to found at Washington, under the name of the Smithsonian Institution, an establishment for the increase and diffusion of knowledge among men." Today, the Smithsonian Institution, charged with the custody of all national collections, is the largest complex of public museums in the world.

The Mall is not the only area of cultural interest in Washington. The Corcoran Gallery of Art, the Phillips Collection, and the Folger Shakespeare Library are only a few of the many fascinating museums scattered throughout the capital city. The National Museum of American Art, the National Portrait Gallery, and the Renwick Gallery of Art, all part of the Smithsonian, are located off the Mall. Among its other facilities, the Smithsonian also administers the John F. Kennedy Center for the Performing Arts in the Foggy Bottom area and the National Zoological Park in Rock Creek Park. However, with seven major museums of the Smithsonian Institution clustered around the Mall, it is small wonder that for many of Washington's visitors, the words *Mall* and *museum* seem almost synonymous.

Here, visitors will find ancient Biblical manuscripts, Chinese bronzes, priceless jewels, First Ladies' ball gowns, George Washington's false teeth, and a live insect zoo. For art lovers, the holdings are equally varied and impressive, from Leonardo da Vinci's *Ginevra de'Benci* to Alexander Calder's 920-pound mobile in the National Gallery's East Wing, a building that is itself like a huge marble sculpture. Approximately nine million people a year visit the Air and Space Museum, the Mall's and the world's most popular museum, to see exhibits that range from the Wright Brothers' plane to the Apollo II spacecraft.

The newest addition to the Smithsonian, a seventy-five-million-dollar underground complex called the "Quadrangle" which houses the Sackler Gallery of Asian Art, an international gallery, and African art, opened in 1987. With the Smithsonian's collection of more than sixty-five million items growing yearly, each successive trip to the Mall promises new experiences, especially during the summer, when the Smithsonian sponsors the open-air Festival of American Folklife, a delightful gathering of folk artists, performers, and musicians from across the country. Fireworks burst overhead on the Fourth of July, but whether you are interested in art, aviation, or Americana, a visit to the Washington Mall can be just as exciting any day of the year.

NATIONAL ARCHIVES. *Behind its six-and-one-half-ton bronze doors are the Declaration of Independence, the Constitution, and the Bill of Rights. Protected from air and harmful light rays, the fragile documents are kept in special helium-filled cases; when not on display, they are lowered into a bombproof vault.*

NATIONAL MUSEUM OF NATURAL HISTORY. *An eight-ton African bush elephant dominates the museum's three-story rotunda. Among the sixty million items in the museum's collection are mastodon and giant ground sloth skeletons, a life-size model of a blue whale, and mounted birds from around the world. One of the most popular items in the Hall of Gems and Minerals is the 45.5-carat Hope Diamond, said to have brought its owners bad luck ever since it was smuggled out of India in the seventeenth century.*

HIRSHHORN MUSEUM AND SCULPTURE GARDEN. *Kenneth Snelson's sixty-foot aluminum* Needle Tower *is one of over 6,000 works of art donated to the nation by self-made millionaire Joseph H. Hirshhorn. The twentieth-century collection, housed in a circular concrete building designed by Gordon Bunshaft, also contains Rodin's* Burghers of Calais, *Moore's* Draped Reclining Figure, *and works by such painters as Miró and Masson.*

NATIONAL AIR AND SPACE MUSEUM. *Some of the missiles on display here are so large that the marble, glass, and steel museum, opened in 1976, had to be built around them. Its "Milestones of Flight" exhibit traces the history of flight from Kitty Hawk to the moon.*

GINEVRA DE'BENCI, WEST BUILDING. *Leonardo da Vinci's painting, acquired through the Ailsa Mellon Bruce Fund, is part of a collection that also includes Botticelli's* Adoration of the Magi, *one of the twenty-one works Andrew Mellon purchased, sight unseen, from the Hermitage in Leningrad.*

WEST BUILDING, NATIONAL GALLERY OF ART *(Upper left). The museum began in the 1930s as a gift to the nation from Andrew Mellon. To encourage contributions from other collectors, Mellon stipulated that the gallery he built not bear his name. The classical building was the work of John Russell Pope, who also designed the Jefferson Memorial.*

EAST BUILDING, NATIONAL GALLERY OF ART *(Lower left). The asymmetrical structure was designed by I. M. Pei to complement its site's unusual trapezoidal shape. The pink marble matches that of the West Building and was mined from the same Tennessee quarry.*

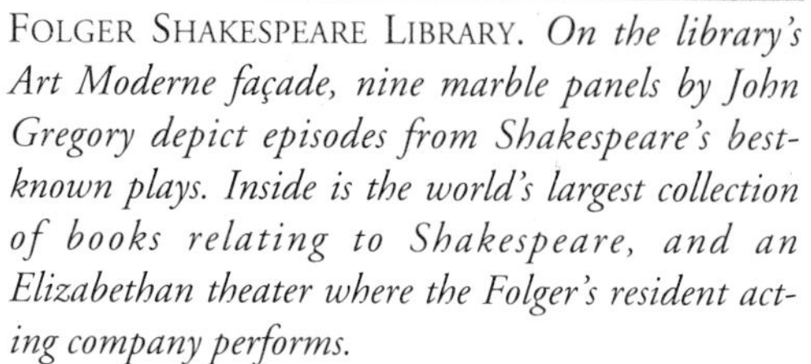

FOLGER SHAKESPEARE LIBRARY. *On the library's Art Moderne façade, nine marble panels by John Gregory depict episodes from Shakespeare's best-known plays. Inside is the world's largest collection of books relating to Shakespeare, and an Elizabethan theater where the Folger's resident acting company performs.*

PHILLIPS COLLECTION. *Pierre Auguste Renoir's* Luncheon of the Boating Party *is perhaps the most famous painting in the nation's first permanent art museum, opened in 1921. Shaped to his personal tastes, Duncan Phillips's collection also includes paintings by Cezanne and Rothko as well as works by artists such as Giorgione and El Greco, whom Phillips regarded as "forever modern."*

JOHN F. KENNEDY CENTER FOR THE PERFORMING ARTS. *The Center's location beneath the noisy flight path to National Airport created special challenges for architect Edward Durrell Stone. Its elaborately soundproofed Opera House, Concert Hall, and Eisenhower Theater are noted for their excellent acoustics.*

GRAND FOYER, KENNEDY CENTER. *Many countries contributed to the capital's only official John F. Kennedy memorial. The eighteen Orrefors crystal chandeliers in the foyer were a gift from Sweden. Italy donated 3,700 tons of marble used in the building's construction.*

City of Monuments

True to L'Enfant's plan for a city of classical grandeur, the capital's most famous monuments—the Washington Monument, the Lincoln Memorial, and the Jefferson Memorial—incorporate architectural motifs from three of the world's great ancient civilizations. The Washington Monument is an Egyptian obelisk, and the Lincoln and Jefferson Memorials echo the Greek Parthenon and the Roman Pantheon, respectively. These elegant marble structures add an aura of timelessness to the capital city. They give the impression of having stood near the banks of the Potomac forever, but this speaks more for the monuments' appearances than it does for their actual ages.

In fact, both the Lincoln and Jefferson Memorials were built after World War I. Even though a monument to the first president was an integral part of L'Enfant's plan, the city's most recognizable landmark was not capped until 1884. When Congress wanted to erect an equestrian statue to honor George Washington in 1783, he vetoed the idea as too extravagant; he seemed far more interested in the establishment of a national church. The site designated in L'Enfant's plan was on Mount Saint Albans, 400 feet above the river, where the Washington National Cathedral now stands.

During the Civil War, when financial constraints halted construction on the Washington Monument, leaving it a 150-foot stump, a less grand, but more poignant memorial was created on the other side of the Potomac. In 1864, the first soldiers were buried in what was to become the Arlington National Cemetery. Established on property that belonged to the family of Robert E. Lee, Arlington National Cemetery contains the graves of two presi-

LINCOLN MEMORIAL *(Above and facing). The thirty-six Doric columns of architect Henry Bacon's neoclassical temple represent the number of states in the Union when Lincoln died. Daniel Chester French spent thirteen years carving the famous nineteen-foot seated figure from interlocking blocks of Georgia marble.*

dents and some 185,000 other Americans who served their country. Since 1921, it has also honored all of America's war dead at the Tomb of the Unknown Soldier, where visitors can witness the changing of the guard every hour on the hour in a simple yet stately ceremony.

The Tomb, a fifty-ton block of white marble inscribed "Here Rests In Honored Glory An American Soldier Known But To God," stands in striking contrast to the Marine Corps War Memorial, a massive bronze statue of six soldiers straining to raise the American flag on the island of Iwo Jima, and the Navy and Marine Memorial, a graceful aluminum sculpture of seven seagulls poised in flight above a cresting wave. But despite their differences, all three spring from a common need, dramatically realized at the capital's newest war monument, the Vietnam Veterans Memorial.

Located in Constitution Gardens near the Reflecting Pool, the Vietnam Veterans Memorial is abstract in design, yet highly personal, for, unique among national war memorials, it lists each of the Americans it honors by name. Dedicated in 1982, the memorial attracts over 100,000 visitors a week. The flags, flowers, and messages Americans leave near the names of their loved ones attest to the power of the black granite monument, one of the most impressive and moving in the city.

NAVY AND MARINE MEMORIAL. *Commonly known as the "Seagull Statue," this elegant sculpture on Columbia Island was designed by Ernesto Begni del Piatta in 1934.*

JEFFERSON MEMORIAL. *John Russell Pope's design incorporates many of Jefferson's favorite architectural motifs. Inside, sculptor Rudulph Evans's nineteen-foot bronze statue depicts Jefferson addressing the Continental Congress.*

WASHINGTON MONUMENT *(Overleaf). When the 555-foot obelisk first opened, it was the world's tallest building. Its elevator was considered too dangerous for women and children, who instead had to climb its 898 steps.*

ARLINGTON NATIONAL CEMETERY *(Above and facing). Although it was intended as a burial ground for the Union dead, the cemetery's first grave was that of a Confederate soldier. Unlike the rounded headstones of most soldiers and sailors, those of Confederates are slightly pointed at the top. Both William Howard Taft and John F. Kennedy are buried here. Major Pierre Charles L'Enfant's grave overlooks the city he planned.*

HEYWOOD
WALKER

VIETNAM VETERANS MEMORIAL. *Built with private donations on land given by the government, it was initiated by Vietnam veteran Jan Scruggs. The long, polished stone wall appears to emerge from and then recede into the earth. The striking design by Maya Ying Lin, then a Yale senior, was selected from 1,421 submissions.*

MARINE CORPS WAR MEMORIAL *(Facing). Based on a Pulitzer Prize-winning photograph by Joseph Rosenthal, Felix de Weldon's powerful bronze work is popularly known as the "Iwo Jima Statue." By special presidential proclamation, its flag flies twenty-four hours a day.*

WASHINGTON NATIONAL CATHEDRAL. *Part of the Episcopal Diocese and officially known as the Cathedral Church of St. Peter and St. Paul, it was chartered by Congress in 1893 as a "House of Prayer for all People" and is essentially interdenominational. Services for such organizations as the United Nations and the armed forces are held here. Construction of the cathedral—an original design in the fourteenth-century English Gothic style—began in 1907 and was completed in 1990.*

ANUM, NATIONAL CATHEDRAL. *wing a plaster cast of a piece d by the sculptor in plasticene, carvers reproduced Frederick* s Ex Nihilo *in place above the ntrance. The magnificent sculp- lepicts mankind's creation from id.*

WINDOW, NORTH TRANSEPT. *ned by Lawrence B. Saint, it con- nore than 9,000 pieces of glass.*

Georgetown & Old Town Alexandria

Georgetown Residence.

One day in 1791, after inspecting the site he had chosen for the Federal District, a discouraged George Washington wrote in his journal, "I derived no great satisfaction from the review." Much of the Potomac River tract was an inhospitable wasteland. However, it did include two considerable assets—the thriving port cities of Alexandria and what was then known as George Town.

Like Alexandria, Georgetown was founded in the mid-1700s on land first settled by Scottish immigrants in the 1670s. It was graced by elegant Georgian and Federal houses bearing witness to prosperity that stemmed from a healthy tobacco trade. The cargo ships that sailed down the Potomac returned from Europe and the West Indies laden with silks, tinware, teas, and wine. In 1800, when the unfinished Capitol and the President's House were surrounded by shantytowns, Georgetown had newspapers, schools, and a university. Like Alexandria, Georgetown was not eager to become part of the capital city, and it petitioned Congress to be returned to the state of Maryland. Its petition was refused. In 1846, Alexandria made a similar petition. Citing the undeniably slow federal development of the area, Alexandria was granted her request and became part of Virginia again.

By this time, Georgetown had fallen into economic decline. In the 1820s, the silting of the Potomac River restricted the port's usefulness. The C & O Canal promised a valuable commercial link between the Chesapeake Bay and the Ohio River Valley, but unfortunately, the canal could not compete with the increasingly efficient railroads. The ambitious project was abandoned 185 miles into construction.

It was not until the 1930s that Georgetown began to regain the prominence it enjoyed in the early years of Washington's history, when Washingtonians found respite in the urbane little city from the rawness of their brand-new capital. Under Franklin Delano Roosevelt's New Deal, unprecedented numbers of federal workers thronged the District of Columbia. The demand for housing was high; so was the interest in preserving America's architectural heritage, and many of Georgetown's older houses were restored or renovated. Gas rationing in World War II made Georgetown's proximity to downtown Washington more attractive than ever, and the neighborhood flourished.

Georgetown has, throughout the years, retained its distinctive character and charm. Since 1950, when the Old Georgetown Act declared the town a National Landmark, great efforts have been made to preserve the façades of Georgetown's eighteenth- and nineteenth-century houses and to assure that the designs of new houses are in harmony with the old. Even though most of Georgetown's fine Federal, Queen Anne, and Victorian houses are not open to the public, annual house and garden tours are popular events.

Rich in history, Georgetown is no museum piece; it boasts some of the trendiest nightspots and pubs in the city. Neighborhood markets, delicatessens, and bookstores are within walking distance; so too are galleries and sophisticated boutiques. Georgetown caters to almost every taste. Both vibrant and serene, it invites tourist and resident alike to stroll in the formal gardens of Dumbarton Oaks, jog along the towpath of the C & O Canal, browse in specialty shops, and dine on international cuisine, all within three miles of Capitol Hill.

Old Town Alexandria Residence.

GEORGET
DUMBARTON
STREET N.W.
CHURCH OF
THE EPIPHANY

ALEXANDRIA, VIRGINIA. *Galleries, boutiques, and restaurants line streets laid out in 1749. With some 400 eighteenth- and early nineteenth-century buildings, Alexandria boasts more original structures than Williamsburg.*

WISCONSIN AVENUE *(Pages 50-51). Representatives from "Au Pied de Cochon" parade with that restaurant's namesake down Georgetown's main street.*

DUMBARTON OAKS.
Principles incorporated in the Charter of the United Nations were drafted here in 1944. Dumbarton Oaks now houses a Center for Byzantine Studies, a Byzantine Museum, and a Pre-Columbian Museum.

PEBBLE GARDEN,
DUMBARTON OAKS
This is one of several self-contained terrace gardens on the sixteen-acre Georgetown estate.

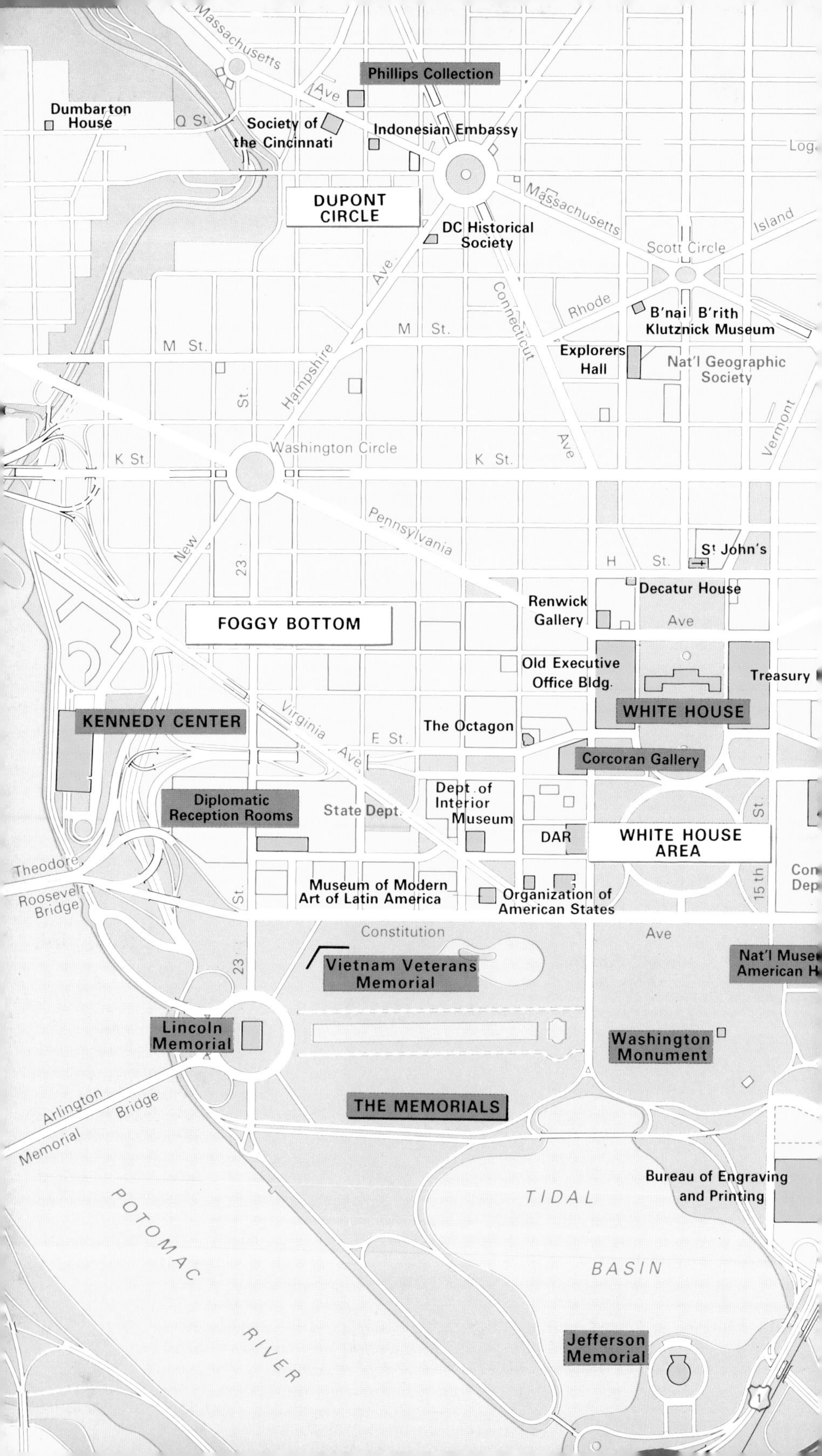

Massachusetts
Ave
Phillips Collection
Dumbarton House
Q St.
Society of the Cincinnati
Indonesian Embassy
Log
DUPONT CIRCLE
Massachusetts
Island
DC Historical Society
Scott Circle
Ave
Connecticut
Rhode
B'nai B'rith Klutznick Museum
M St.
M St.
Explorers Hall
Nat'l Geographic Society
Hampshire
St.
Vermont
Washington Circle
K St.
K St.
Ave
Pennsylvania
New
23
H St.
St John's
Decatur House
Renwick Gallery
Ave
FOGGY BOTTOM
Old Executive Office Bldg.
Treasury
WHITE HOUSE
KENNEDY CENTER
Virginia
Ave
E St.
The Octagon
Corcoran Gallery
Diplomatic Reception Rooms
State Dept.
Dept. of Interior Museum
St.
DAR
WHITE HOUSE AREA
Theodore Roosevelt Bridge
St.
Museum of Modern Art of Latin America
Organization of American States
15th
Constitution
Ave
Vietnam Veterans Memorial
23
Lincoln Memorial
Washington Monument
Arlington Memorial Bridge
THE MEMORIALS
Bureau of Engraving and Printing
TIDAL
BASIN
POTOMAC
RIVER
Jefferson Memorial
1

MAP OF
KEY ATTRACTIONS
WASHINGTON, D.C.
500 m
0
152 ft
Island Ave.
New Jersey Ave.
7 St.
M St.
New York Ave.
M St
Capitol
Mt Vernon Square
K St.
K St.
North
Tech 2000
Capital Children's Museum
DOWNTOWN
H St.
Nat'l Museum of American Art
Nat'l Bldg Museum
Massachusetts Ave
Union Station
Nat'l Portrait Gallery
d's Theatre
E St
5th St.
7th St.
Ave
Ave
CAPITOL HILL
Hart Bldg.
National Archives
Louisiana Ave
Sewall-Belmont House
Constitution Ave
Supreme Court
National Gallery of Art
CAPITOL
1st St.
Madison Dr.
East Capitol St.
Nat'l Air and Space Museum
Folger Shakespeare Library
Jefferson Dr.
US Botanic Garden
LIBRARY OF CONGRESS
Independence Ave
Hirshhorn Museum
Arts and Industries Bldg.
New Jersey Ave
5th St.
St.
395
Southwest Freeway
7th

M metro **System Map**

Legend

- Red Line • Glenmont/ Shady Grove
- Orange Line • New Carrollton/ Vienna
- Blue Line • Addison Road/ Franconia-Springfield
- Green Line • Branch Avenue/ Greenbelt
- Yellow Line • Huntington/ Mt Vernon Sq-UDC

MARC Commuter Rail
Parking
Station in service

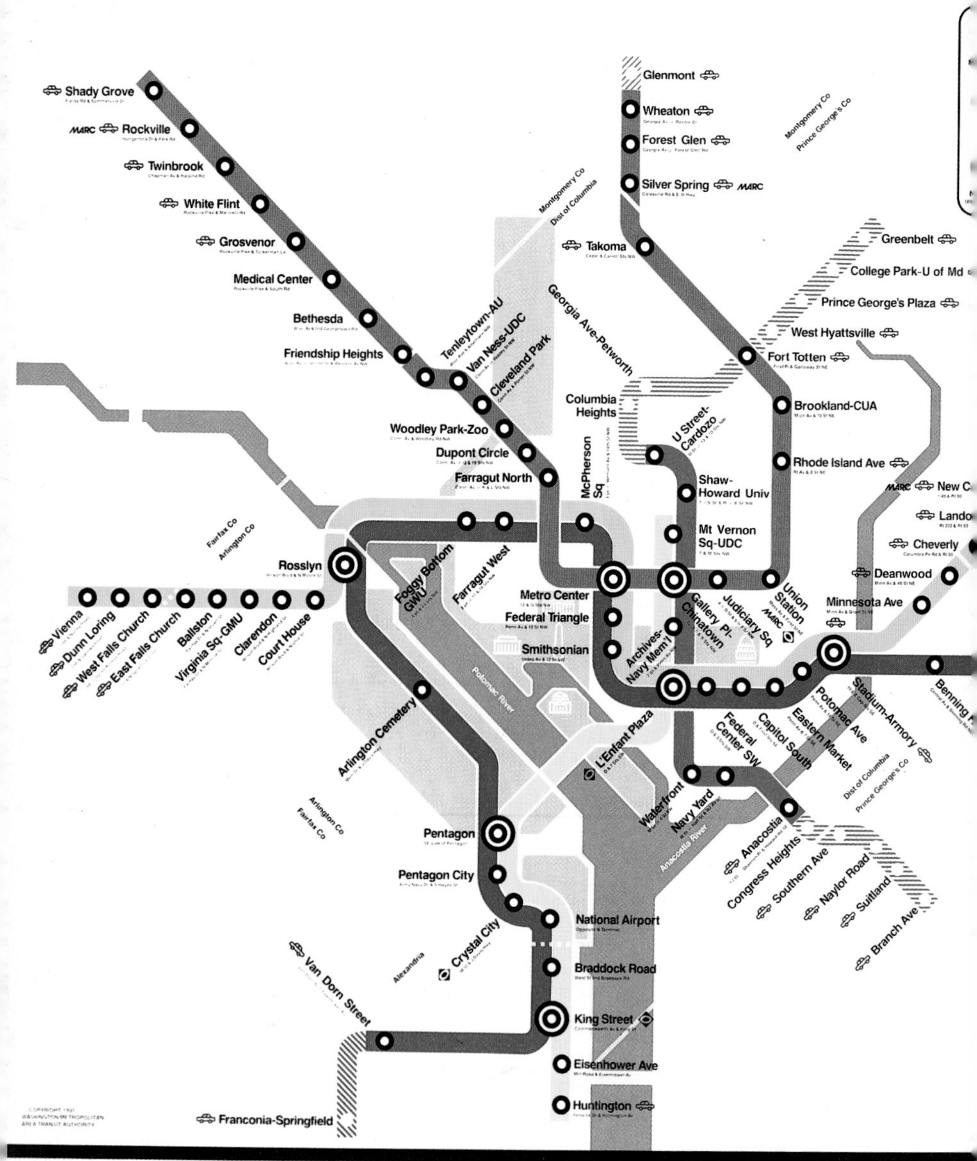

Map courtesy of the Washington Metropolitan Area Transit Authority.

Printed and bound in the United States.

00 99 98 97 96 95 94 93 5 4 3 2 1

Any inquiries should be directed to Thomasson-Grant, Inc.
One Morton Drive, Suite 500, Charlottesville, Virginia
22903-6806 , telephone (804) 977-1780.

Principal photography by Charles Shoffner.
Additional photographs:
Pages 1, 2-3, 13, 22-23, and 34-35, Robert Llewellyn.
Pages 8, 10, 20, 24, 25, 40-41, and cover, John F. Grant.
Page 14, Richard Cheek.
Page 17, Carol M. Highsmith.
Page 29, National Gallery of Art, Washington.
Page 31, The Phillips Collection, Washington.
Pages 50-51, Fred Maroon.
Back cover, © 1993 Jack Mellott.